Walking Sacred Lands

Poems by

Catherine Veritas

ISBN- 10 : 0-9913638-5-x
ISBN-13 : 978-0-9913638-5-8

Cover design by H.O. Charles
Cover Photo by Helena Brandfors

Verita Holma Press

CatherineVeritas.com
Pahoa, Hawaii

Dedicated with gratitude to the women, men,
and children of Hawai'i.

In appreciation and memory of
Kumu Victoria Marie Far Heong Ng

Author's Note

Three poems in this collection are paired with my Hawaiian translations. Although I am a beginning level student, I choose to include them, 'e kala mai to fluent speakers of 'olelo Hawai'i, because the beauty of the language outweighs my awkwardness of phrasing, and because the words express my respect and aloha for ka mo'olelo Hawai'i.

Special thanks to Cheryl Carroll, Libby Pulelehua Oshiyama, Helena Brandfors, and the family of Kumu Victoria Ng.

Table of Contents

Walking Sacred Lands

I Live Inside a Miracle

I live inside a miracle
so do you
if you're alive
if you're reading this
it's already true!
you, me, words, meaning
miracles
beauty, decay, birth, death
miracles
this
alive
moment
let it overwhelm you
let it melt you
into surrender
into laughter
into everything
surrender, laughter, everything
miracles

Gathering

What is your story
when were you called
how did she snatch you from your ordered life
demanding attendance
did she sweet-talk you
seducing you closer and closer
until you heaved yourself across oceans
with all your might
did she enter you like an earthquake
rattling and dismantling
old-world structures
forcing you to rebuild a new
internal design
or maybe you were the lucky duck
gliding to Hawai'i Island on a rainbow bridge
singing "wee, wee, wee" all the way home
however brought
ko'u mau hoaloha
my friends
devotees of Pele
and each other
we form a raucous harmony
how amazing
how lucky
are we

Ko'u Kuamo'o

I.
I carry a dragon upon my back
she is quick of wit
and survival-fit
oh somedays how she quivers and flails
spine bristling
tail swooshing
fire and steam at the ready
she takes me for a ride
those days
I am lost inside an untamed beast

II.
You are never lost
the wise sage says
here
is where you are
dancing with your dragon's power
here
is where to call the light
to help you find your way
to love her
your dragon
innocent and fierce in her desire to protect you
whom she dearly loves
consider this
love her fire
and her instinct

find the essence in her wants and needs
embrace her
as a part of your beautiful self
together you will fly

Kuamo'o is the Hawaiian word for spine/backbone
Kua   - to bear
Mo'o - lizard, serpent, dragon

Invisible Path

Bewildering
my choice
to walk this invisible path
through forests deep
swamps sticky with quicksand
over difficult mountain passes
don't watch me too closely
for I do not know what it is I follow
if you ask
I'll stammer fragments of an ancient prayer
at night
by starlight
or moonlight
I mull remembered passages
weave new words into old
wait
and wonder
in the morning
I rise again
the invisible path leads forward
into a brand new day

Volcano

I am volcano
anger
want
frustration
envy
swirl inside me
beneath me
a cauldron of fire
deeper still
I feel the world's pain
inexhaustible causes of suffering
I want to explode
ease the pain
implode
squelch the fury
or remain
bearing this red well of churning
burning
this uncomfortable fuel
learning
new ways
to transform density
dark intensity
from suffering
into light

Once There Was a Woman Stuck in Grief

Once there was a woman who was stuck in grief
she mourned her ex-lover ten years
her dead cat another ten
her dear teacher
ahead of time
because he would one day die
regarding patients and loved ones
she recounted countless moments of their pains and
fears
hurting with each
she was a woman stuck in grief
moving through days of beautiful service and
friendship
with a tear behind her eye
a veil over her thoughts

then along came Power
she met Power on a visit to the volcano
it was the time of the woman's changing
from child-bearer to crone
(her own fires stirring)
I eat grief Pele of the volcano told her
I am big enough
strong enough
wild enough
to consume any emotion you offer

the woman felt sudden relief
and then hope
so a change began
not just then
but soon
a door opened here
a push came from over there
an address
an invitation
a vision formed
the woman moved to Pele's land of Power
shipping all she owned across the pacific sea
when she set up her new household
and opened the box she had marked "Grief"
oh the demons and wonders she found inside
fear anger judgment doubt poured out
entangled and entwined with her grief
and underneath
at the bottom of her Pandora's box
swaddled
protected
a precious, young part of herself
the woman scarcely knew how to tend
that tender part
her home so filled with strong emotions
it was hard even to not lose sight

she reminded herself
this is a place of Power
greater than her Pandora's box
of flowing feelings
she knew (she prayed)
despite fear anger judgment doubt
that she was ready willing
humble enough
to tame
embrace
and celebrate
all her tender and unruly parts
under the shadow of Pele's volcano

Kilauea Caldera

To the altar of your caldera
I have brought a willing sacrifice
myself
wisdom and ignorance
effort and dreams
I lay my offering beside
abundant
earnest
gifts
left by pilgrims before me
brave souls
from near
and far
drawn to the mystery
of your creative
destructive
magnetic
fire

My Life Is Perfection as a Work of Art

My life is perfection
as a work of art
lo, dramatic tension in every shape and form
witness love and fear dance together
on the head of a pin
pay rapt attention to the battle
between judgment and freedom
creating a sense of perpetual motion
note the swirling knot of contrasts
at the center of the frame
one could never be bored
living a life such as this
was this the artist's intention?
and who is said artist anyway?

The Secret of Flight

I witness
as you launch yourself
into the great tumult
my quiet questions scarcely register
so loud the roiling in your ears
your face
a blissful countenance
your mind
focused on freedom
release
the promise of soul-mate love
one foot is stretched across the abyss
angels be with you
perhaps you know
the secret of flight

The Honeymoon Is Over

The honeymoon is over
how long did yours last
two weeks?
two years?
I suppose I can claim a lucky seven
but finally
the honeymoon is over
the marriage dance begins
maybe you thought it all fun and games
sex
playing house
a nice escort to family functions
but here
now
the real deal
the steady remolding of the soul
how could life combine such a perfect pair
intricate jigsaw of complimentary gifts
shared dreams
and conflicting styles
how could the mystery of coupling
draw my body
toward an "other"
and make me stay long enough
for secret judgements and karmic hurts
to be exposed to the light of day

the compassion of the heart
unearthing mind-expanding realms
of freedom
how could I like someone long enough
and be loved back hard enough
to tolerate
the "why are we here?" times
the competing and bickering times
and be soul-smiling glad I did
we are here
together
growing something greater than us
something is being born through us
(higher selves
perhaps)
look around
see what has been born in your time together
celebrate the births
evolutions
accomplishments
there will be new honeymoons
you will delight at their arrival
and the marriage dance will continue
one, two, trip, bounce, twirl
one, two, drag, leap, let go

A Rising Tide Lifts All Boats

I am generating an ocean of goodness
great enough to lift all boats
yours
mine
the child mourning in Brussels
the homeless vet in a wheelchair
my ocean is yet
just a drop
barely enough to wet my toes
but I imagine my beneficence
IMMENSE
if I can only mind my mind
wish well for all beings at all times
a bucket of my tears here
sweat of my labor there
I do what I can
to generate an ocean of goodness
finally
my ocean is big enough to fit both my feet
I step inside
wish my tender-hearted self well
surprise
opening my lids
I see with new eyes
an ocean of goodness spreading
in every direction

Anytime You're Ready

My mind says
when you're ready to go forward
without going backward
(in self-judgment or regret)
let me know

my husband says
when you're ready to move forward
without going backward
(with excuses or blame)
let me know

God says
when you're ready to move forward
without reaching back
when you're ready to live this freedom
taste this tingling aliveness
I'm here
anytime you're ready
it's good
going backward
is fine too
but when you're ready
notice

I am here

all around you

see how I hold you
see how I give you
everything

*God: The Universe; Great Mother; Field of
All Possibility; Great Spirit; Higher Power; Life

The Joke On Me

Ha ha
the joke is on me
I rushed forth
with the fervor of an acolyte
to follow my heart to Pele
a real Goddess!
as real as the formation of the planet
as fire and molten rock
as real as any modern woman could hope
to behold
I came to live a spiritual life
in this place of lovingly-tended Power
I made no bargain mind you
I simply stood before her
bowing inwardly
reverently
compelled by a craving
to relate to Power
greater than Awe
what did I expect
for my leap of faith
that I would be singled out
and sympathetically empowered?
er, yes
that I would find new purpose
inwardly thrilling
and outwardly inspiring?
ha ha

I surrendered the comfort of a familiar life
(and pains too heavy to carry forward)
then wondered why
I found myself
dissolving
into the length of days
slow timelessness of rain
I imagined a "spiritual life"
in a mystical land
only to discover
my path is to sweep floors
with pleasant cheer
wash dishes
without resentment
clean the ever-growing mold
grapple with untamable vines
is this why I rushed here?
to be a house-wife
a jungle weed-er
a kind neighbor
oh
reality check
desire for a spiritual life
might be answered
in ways not imagined

simple chores
accomplished with peaceful thoughts
awareness of breath
in the wee hours
of sleepless middle-age nights
the sound of rain
the whistling of frogs

Kindness

I am kindness inside sorrow
I am kindness inside peace
I am the kindness inside my heart

I am kindness inside confusion
I am kindness inside this electro-magnetic soup
I am kindness inside my heart

I am kindness that doesn't care
who you are
where you stand
what we have or have not done
I am kindness inside my heart

Twenty-four Hours

Twenty-four brand new hours
to be in awe of reality
twenty-four brand new hours
to set myself free
twenty-four brand new hours
to "want what God wants"
twenty-four brand new hours
to love

*Quote from Byron Katie. Inspiration from Thich Nhat Hahn.

A New Day

No boss is raging
no mother berating
no child is dying
no mortgage overdue
and still
the FEAR
will appear
I say I love God
then see the world as a threat
life as karmic avenger
ready to punish any debt
it's crazy
the adrenaline I have to transmute every day
it might surprise you to know
for I seem calm and gay
I can meditate, pray, therapize, and exercise
and still
doubt will arise
ready to take that amusement park spin
from thought to worry to fear again
I wish it wasn't so hard
to ride my waves of emotion
when peace and love
are my desire and devotion
left to its own hypersensitive devices
my nervous system acts as if life
is a serial crisis

I begrudge that I'm prone
to both fear and melancholy
I judge this angst
I judge it as folly
and then
and then
the tide will shift
the moon will lift
I remember the teachings, the insights
the beauty
I know I belong
my breath pulls deep and long
it makes me wonder if the now is a trick
if I could only remember which switch to flick
perhaps it's a state I can better-learn to create
like a mellow mood
or a soulful groove
see I'm here and then I'm there
in this pendulum swing
what to do I ask
how can joy really take wing
some of the teachings still hum in my head
rather than fretting now I'll try one instead
love the fear
love delight
love the doubt

love the night
love this chair
love this dare
love the cat's allergenic hair
I don't know if there's a teaching
that will completely heal my mind
so to my dear emotional-self
I vow best effort to be kind
succeed or fail
at this task either way
tomorrow
is always
a new
day

Lojong Slogan #32

Lojong is a Buddhist mind training practice consisting of 59 slogans—"antidotes to the undesired mental habits that cause suffering."

Some slogans are obvious
"don't talk about injured limbs"
others cryptic
"don't turn gods into demons"
but slogan 32
"don't wait in ambush"
got to me
embarrassingly
the heel of a boot splashing into a mud puddle
I could pretend it hadn't just splattered
my new pretty slacks
but I was marked
initially slogan 32 sounded in my brain
like the thud of low-C on a child's xylophone set
before the week was out
slogan 32 had become
an insistent purple chiming high-C
I'll tell him how he hurt my feelings
chime
I'll try not to raise my voice and I'll say
chime chime
it was unfair

"don't wait in ambush"

why should I take counsel
from an ancient mind training slogan
I'm being rational here
taking care of my feelings
right?
amazingly
I heard an inner voice reply

come on up to a higher plateau
a few steps up you get a whole new view
feel those emotions churning inside?
let that tantrum not be your business for a while
something got wound up
(brain chemistry, childhood dynamics, star
alignments)
and needs to tire itself out
sit with me here
where the air is clear and you can see for miles
so fresh
it makes your eyes smile
look again at your upset
see how little it matters from up here
maybe you misconstrued that a tone of voice could
be a reason for war

maybe you got caught in ego's hall of mirrors
or thought it your job to keep the score
let's wait here
a little above the fracas
pondering impermanence
and eternity
you will go back with a fresh mind
trust yourself
to meet the moment that arises
the next new surprise
with compassion and honesty
with clear, awake eyes

Thank You For Sharing

Regret
thank you for your colorful story
I release you now
worry
thank you for your provocative concern
perhaps we'll discuss it later
criticism
thank you for your clever comments
goodbye to you
as well

what
remains
in this quiet space
is love
I
am love
listening
for love

Dancing in the Dark

I've faced my fear
gentled my anger
transformed envy
outwitted despair
but now
scariest of all
stepping down intellect
from command and control
mind oh brilliant mind
honed and strengthened
with each challenge faced
I love you
I thank you
but no thanks just now
I'm dancing in the dark
flowing with the tides
navigating by feel
witnessing the signs
trusting
life, Herself
to guide me home

No Need To Judge

There's no need
to judge
to compare
or understand this moment

stop
breathe
smile if you can

notice the love
the mystery
the body's impulse toward movement
or stillness

be this truth
live this moment
now

"Delete the need to judge, to compare, to understand," from the teaching of William Brugh Joy M.D.

Shaman to Spirit Guide

Sink me into quicksand
tie me to a tree
take away my legs
remove my head
how many different ways
did you tell me
to stop seeking
to wait
schemes and expectations falling away
be still
and wait
I wait in sunlight
I wait in the dark
I wait in rain
I wait in rain's passing
before my eyes
beauty becomes magnified
all around
laughter and love resound
from above
light descends
soon you will see me shining
radiant as the sun

Vertical Time

Vertical time
beyond the mind time
old soul time
immoveable strength time
deeps of the earth time
honor the ancestors time
all is well time
I am you time
vertical time

"Vertical time" is a teaching of lineage kahuna Harry
Uhane Jim, from his book *Wise Secrets of Aloha*.

Nani Loa

Nani loa i keia la
mahalo
makemake au i ho'opilialoha
me keia la
makemake au i he pilialoha
me na wahine, na kane, a na keiki o Hawai'i
makemake au i 'ike ka 'aina
a aloha ka 'aina
nani loa i keia la
ho'oikaika keia manawa 'o au
mahalo

'amama ua noa

Very Beautiful

This day is very beautiful
thank you
I want to make a loving relationship
with this day
I want to make loving relationships
with the women, men, and children of Hawaii
I want to know the land
and love the land
this day is very beautiful
this moment
makes me strong
thank you

this prayer is released

Translation from previous page

Pueo

Dusk
turns to night
Pueo watches
and waits
but does not enter the space

spidery cracks bloom across my slick surface
thaw has begun
form steadily melts into formlessness
I seep into receptive Earth

bulldozers rev
I am helpless to halt
the scraping crushing treads
ripping Earth's crust

in aftermath
I am not wounded by the desecration
for my essence has retreated
deeper still

I am willing to not be form
I am willing to not be resistance
I am willing to not be my own story
of transformation

only then does Pueo enter the space

wings unfurl
nook and cranny are filled with silver light
owl light
moon light
shimmering from every tufted feather

I am reborn
in the benediction
of Pueo's presence
in the space of my absence

gratitude

peace

Pueo is the Hawaiian owl,
one of the forms assumed by Hawaiian ancestor
spirits.

I Tremble Before Tradition

I tremble before tradition
before the ancestors
before the spirits of this land
yet here you are
calling me
teasing me
speaking to me
ancestors, seen and unseen
gods of the forty thousand places and things
you exist
immersed in the power of the land
nourished by the reverence of a people
I tremble with awe and hesitation
today I give you my name
toss it upon your winds
do what you will
my heart is already committed
to our engagement

Ha'alulu Au I Ke Alo O Ka Mo'olelo

Ha'alulu au i ke alo o ka mo'olelo
i ke alo o na kupuna
a na akua o ka 'aina
na'e eia oukou
kahea oukou ia'u
henehene ia'u
olelo ia'u
na kupuna, kumaka a kumaka 'ole
kini o ke akua
e ola mau
pulu 'oukou ma ka mana o ka 'aina
ko'o 'oukou me ke aloha no na kanaka
ha'alulu au me e'ehia a kanalua
ha'awi manawale'a a'u ko'u inoa i keia la
ho'olele 'oukou 'ia ma ka makani
e malama 'ia ko 'oukou makemake
ua ho'oko au ana
i kakou pilina

Translation from previous page

Ke Akua, Na Akua

Ke Akua
na akua
the One God
the many spirits of the land
where one stands
'Io
Jah
Jehova Rapha
Jehova Jireh
in one Creation
many Names
what can we do
but pray
for wisdom
and love one another
while the mind questions
na'au recognizes Oneness
beyond understanding
Ke Akua
Source and Completion of all
that has ever existed
and will ever exist
every story dreamed
every grace received
every power named

every tiny
colorful
secret
or bold part
of this Great Mystery

na'au - inner wisdom; knowing of the gut and heart

Pa'a

Steady in rushing waters
pa'a
in wave's froth and pull
pa'a
inside mind's confusion
pa'a
as expectations fall away
hold to the core
pa'a

Pa'a is connection to the earth, groundedness,
conscious presence, steadfastness.

Halo

My hair is on fire
light is my heart's desire
into darkness I shine
this light is divine

Transplant

I am rooting in this place
maturing
growing old
stories flow around me
like water
like wind
land flows inside me
like nectar
like sap
I am rooting in this place
maturing
growing old

Dare

Rest your eyes
in their sockets
rest your mind
on your heart
rest your heart
into a cozy sweet place
while resting your heels
in a cool mountain stream
now
rest your will
into God's
for as long as you dare

Prayer

Thank you for this day on the garden planet
thank you for life
for love in all its flavors
for the worthy challenge of being human
help me remember my union with that
which gives rise to this world
my union with fire
and rock
and Gaia's sacred heart within
spread forgiveness
for the errors of humanity
as we seek our way through all that surrounds us
and continue to heal us
thrill us
amaze us
with the beauty of creation

Pule No Ke Akua Nui

Mahalo no keia la ma ka hoku mala pua
mahalo no ke ola
no ke aloha
no ka ʻaʻa ʻana i keia mea he nohona kanaka
hoʻomanaʻo mai ko makou pilina i ke kumulipo no
keia honua
ko makou pilina i ke ahi
me ka pohaku
a me ka naʻau ʻo Papa
uhola i kala nei i na hewa o na kanaka
ʻoiai ʻimi makou i ke ala e puni ana makou
hoʻomau ʻOe lapaʻau mai ia makou
hoʻoilihia ia makou
me ka nani loa no ke ao holokoʻa

Translation from previous page

Ode to My Feet

My heart is true
but the colors it wears
distract my eye
from the truth it bears
my mind it plans
ruminates
remembers
believes
questions
then surrenders
but my feet
I trust to know the deal
stay put
or move toward what is real
to my feet I say
deep love
thank you
I adore the fabulous pair of you
we've been hurt
we've healed
we've taken stands
now we're grounded in earthly mystery
walking sacred lands

Catherine Veritas practices art, healing, and tutoring children on Hawai'i Island. For more than 30 years she served as a Holistic Chiropractor in West Los Angeles, California, before moving to Hawaii in 2015. She is the author of *The Maltese Dreamer*, a novel, and *At My Heart a Turquoise Lake*, a book of poetry.

www.CatherineVeritas.com

www.ingramcontent.com/pod-product-compliance
Lightning Source LLC
Chambersburg PA
CBHW060723030426
42337CB00017B/2986